e. e. cummings

*was born in Cambridge, Massachusetts, in
1894. He attended Harvard where his father
had been an assistant professor of English.
In World War I, he went to France as an
ambulance driver and later served as a private in the American Army. It was during
his French experience that he wrote*
The Enormous Room *and with it achieved
a measure of popularity.*

*After the war he studied art in Paris. In
1925 he won the* Dial *prize and, in 1928, his
play,* him, *was produced by the Province-
town Players. Since then Cummings has
produced a steady flow of poetry and paint-
ings. He is a member of the National In-
stitute of Arts and Letters, and in 1955 he
received a special citation from the National Book Awards committee for his*
Poems, *1923-1954.*

*Cummings has written this about his
poetry: "So far as I am concerned, poetry
and every other art was and is and forever
will be strictly and distinctly a question of
individuality. . . . If poetry is your goal,
you've got to forget all about punishments
and all about rewards and all about self-
styled obligations and duties and responsi-
bilities etcetera ad infinitum and remember
one thing only: that it's you — nobody else
— who determine your destiny and decide
your fate."*

50

POEMS

E. E. Cummings

The Universal Library
GROSSET & DUNLAP
NEW YORK

to m. m.

Some of the poems in this book have appeared in *Furioso*, *Poetry*, and *Poetry Weekly*. Grateful acknowledgment is made for permission to reprint them.

INDEX OF FIRST LINES

POEMS

!blac
k
agains
t

(whi)

te sky
?t
rees whic
h fr

om droppe

d

,
le
af

a:;go

e
s wh
IrlI
n

.g

fl

a
tt
ene

d d

reaml
essn
esse

s wa

it
sp
i

t)(t

he
s
e

f

ooli
sh sh
apes

ccocoucougcoughcoughi

ng with me
n more o
n than in the

m

3

If you can't eat you got to

smoke and we aint got
nothing to smoke:come on kid

let's go to sleep
if you can't smoke you got to

Sing and we aint got

nothing to sing;come on kid
let's go to sleep

if you can't sing you got to
die and we aint got

Nothing to die,come on kid

let's go to sleep
if you can't die you got to

dream and we aint got
nothing to dream(come on kid

Let's go to sleep)

4

nobody loved this
he)with its
of eye stuck
into a rock of

forehead.No
body

loved
big that quick
sharp
thick snake of a

voice these

root
like legs
or
feethands;

nobody
ever could ever

had love loved whose his
climbing shoulders queerly twilight
:never,no
(body.

Nothing

am was. are leaves few this. is these a or
scratchily over which of earth dragged once
-ful leaf. & were who skies clutch an of poor
how colding hereless. air theres what immense
live without every dancing. singless only a child's eyes float silently down
more than two those that and that noing our
gone snow gone
     yours mine
        . We're
alive and shall be:cities may overflow(am
was)assassinating whole grassblades,five
ideas can swallow a man;three words im
-prison a woman for all her now:but we've
such freedom such intense digestion so
much greenness only dying makes us grow

6

flotsam and jetsam
are gentlemen poeds
urseappeal netsam
our spinsters and coeds)

thoroughly bretish
they scout the inhuman
itarian fetish
that man isn't wuman

vive the millenni
um three cheers for labor
give all things to enni
one bugger thy nabor

(neck and senecktie
are gentlemen ppoyds
even whose recktie
are covered by lloyd's

moan
(is)
ing

the she of the
sea
un

der a who
a he a moon a
magic out

of the black this which of
one street leaps quick
squirmthicklying lu

minous night
mare som
e w

hereanynoevery
ing(danc)ing
wills&weres

8

the Noster was a ship of swank
(as gallant as they come)
until she hit a mine and sank
just off the coast of Sum

precisely where a craft of cost
the Ergo perished later
all hands(you may recall)being lost
including captain Pater

warped this perhapsy
stumbl
i
 NgflounderpirouettiN
                        g

:seized(

tatterdemalion
dow
     nupfloatsw
                  oon
InG

s ly)tuck.s its(ghostsoul sheshape)

elf into leasting forever most
magical maybes of certainly
never the iswas

teetertiptotterish

sp-
   inwhirlpin
              -wh
EEling
;a!who,

(

whic hbubble ssomethin
gabou tlov
e)

spoke joe to jack

leave her alone
she's not your gal

jack spoke to joe
's left crashed
pal dropped

o god alice
yells but who shot
up grabbing had
by my throat me

give it him good
a bottle she
quick who stop damned
fall all we go spill

and chairs tables the and
bitch whispers jill
mopping too bad

dear sh not yet
jesus what blood

darling i said

red-rag and pink-flag
blackshirt and brown
strut-mince and stink-brag
have all come to town

some like it shot
and some like it hung
and some like it in the twot
nine months young

(will you teach a
wretch to live
straighter than a needle)

ask
    her
        ask
            when
                (ask and
                ask
                and ask
again and)ask a
brittle little
person fiddling
in
the
rain

(did you kiss
a girl with nipples
like pink thimbles)

ask
    him
        ask
            who
                (ask and
                ask
                and ask
ago and)ask a
simple
crazy
thing
singing
in the snow

proud of his scientific attitude

and liked the prince of wales wife wants to die
but the doctors won't let her comma considers frood
whom he pronounces young mistaken and
cradles in rubbery one somewhat hand
the paper destinies of nations sic
item a bounceless period unshy
the empty house is full O Yes of guk
rooms daughter item son a woopsing queer
colon hobby photography never has plumbed
the heights of prowst but respects artists if
they are sincere proud of his scientif
ic attitude and liked the king of)hear

ye!the godless are the dull and the dull are the damned

14

the way to hump a cow is not
to get yourself a stool
but draw a line around the spot
and call it beautifool

to multiply because and why
dividing thens by nows
and adding and(i understand)
is hows to hump a cows

the way to hump a cow is not
to elevate your tool
but drop a penny in the slot
and bellow like a bool

to lay a wreath from ancient greath
on insulated brows
(while tossing boms at uncle toms)
is hows to hump a cows

the way to hump a cow is not
to push and then to pull
but practicing the art of swot
to preach the golden rull

to vote for me(all decent mem
and wonens will allows
which if they don't to hell with them)
is hows to hump a cows

mrs

& mr across the way are kind of
afraid)afraid

of what(of

a crazy man)don't
ask me how i know(a he of head
comes to some dirty window every)twilight i

feel(his lousy eyes roaming)wonderful all

sky(a little mouth)stumbling(can't
keep up with how big very
them)now(it tears
off rag its

of

mind chucks away flimsy
which but)always(they're
more much further off)further these
those three disappear finally what's left

behind is(just a head of he

is)merely(a pair of ears with some
lips plus a couple of)holes probably that's what
(mr & mrs are

sort of really

really kind
of afraid of)these(down pull & who'll

shades

)when what hugs stopping earth than silent is
more silent than more than much more is or
total sun oceaning than any this
tear jumping from each most least eye of star

and without was if minus and shall be
immeasurable happenless unnow
shuts more than open could that every tree
or than all life more death begins to grow

end's ending then these dolls of joy and grief
these recent memories of future dream
these perhaps who have lost their shadows if
which did not do the losing spectres mime

until out of merely not nothing comes
only one snowflake(and we speak our names

youful

larger
of smallish)

Humble a
rosily
,nimblest;

c-urlin-g
noworld
Silent is

blue
(sleep!new

girlgold

ecco a letter starting "dearest we"
unsigned:remarkably brief but covering
one complete miracle of nearest far

"i cordially invite me to become
noone except yourselves r s v p"

she cannot read or write,la moon. Employs
a very crazily how clownlike that
this quickly ghost scribbling from there to where

—name unless i'm mistaken chauvesouris—
whose grammar is atrocious;but so what

princess selene doesn't know a thing
who's much too busy being her beautiful yes.
The place is now
                    let us accept
                              (the time

forever,and you'll wear your silver shoes

there is a here and

that here was a
town(and the town is

so aged the ocean
wanders the streets are so
ancient the houses enter the

people are so feeble the feeble go to
sleep if the people sit down)
and this light is so dark the mountains
grow up from

the sky is so near the earth does not
open her
eyes(but the
feeble are people the feeble
are so wise the people

remember being born)
when and
if nothing disappears they
will disappear always who are filled

with never are more than
more is are mostly
almost are feebler than feeble are

fable who are less than these are least is who
are am(beyond when behind where under

un)

harder perhaps than a newengland bed

these ends of arms which pinch that purple book
between what hands had been before they died

squirming:now withered and unself her gnarled
vomits a rock of mindscream into life;
possibly darker than a spinster's heart

my voice feels who inquires is your cough
better today?nn-nn went head face goes

(if how begins a pillow's green means face

or why a quilt's pink stops might equal head).
Then with the splendor of an angel's fart

came one trembling out of huge each eye look
"thank you" nicely the lady's small grin said
(with more simplicity than makes a world)

six

are in a room's dark around)
five

(are all dancesing singdance all are

three
with faces made of cloud dancing and
three
singing with voices made of earth and

six are in a room's dark around)

five
(six are in a room's)
one

is red

and(six are in)
four are

white

(three singdance six dancesing three
all around around all
clouds singing three and
and three dancing earths

three menandwomen three

and all around all and
all around five all
around five around)

five flowers five

(six are in a room's dark)
all five are one

flowers five flowers and all one is fire

nouns to nouns

wan
wan

too nons two

and
and

nuns two nuns

w an d
ering

in sin

g
ular untheknowndulous s

pring

a pretty a day
(and every fades)
is here and away
(but born are maids
to flower an hour
in all,all)

o yes to flower
until so blithe
a doer a wooer
some limber and lithe
some very fine mower
a tall;tall

some jerry so very
(and nellie and fan)
some handsomest harry
(and sally and nan
they tremble and cower
so pale:pale)

for betty was born
to never say nay
but lucy could learn
and lily could pray
and fewer were shyer
than doll. doll

24

these people socalled were not given hearts
how should they be?their socalled hearts would think
these socalled people have no minds but if
they had their minds socalled would not exist

but if these not existing minds took life
such life could not begin to live id est
breathe but if such life could its breath would stink

and as for souls why souls are wholes not parts
but all these hundreds upon thousands of
people socalled if multiplied by twice
infinity could never equal one)

which may your million selves and my suffice
to through the only mystery of love
become while every sun goes round its moon

as freedom is a breakfastfood
or truth can live with right and wrong
or molehills are from mountains made
—long enough and just so long
will being pay the rent of seem
and genius please the talentgang
and water most encourage flame

as hatracks into peachtrees grow
or hopes dance best on bald men's hair
and every finger is a toe
and any courage is a fear
—long enough and just so long
will the impure think all things pure
and hornets wail by children stung

or as the seeing are the blind
and robins never welcome spring
nor flatfolk prove their world is round
nor dingsters die at break of dong
and common's rare and millstones float
—long enough and just so long
tomorrow will not be too late

worms are the words but joy's the voice
down shall go which and up come who
breasts will be breasts thighs will be thighs
deeds cannot dream what dreams can do
—time is a tree(this life one leaf)
but love is the sky and i am for you
just so long and long enough

wherelings whenlings
(daughters of ifbut offspring of hopefear
sons of unless and children of almost)
never shall guess the dimension of

him whose
each
foot likes the
here of this earth

whose both
eyes
love
this now of the sky

—endlings of isn't
shall never
begin
to begin to

imagine how(only are shall be were
dawn dark rain snow rain
-bow &
a

moon
's whis-
per
in sunset

or thrushes toward dusk among whippoorwills or
tree field rock hollyhock forest brook chickadee
mountain. Mountain)
whycoloured worlds of because do

not stand against yes which is built by
forever & sunsmell
(sometimes a wonder
of wild roses

sometimes)
with north
over
the barn

buy me an ounce and i'll sell you a pound.
Turn
gert
      (spin!
helen)the
slimmer the finger the thicker the thumb(it's
whirl,
girls)
round and round

early to better is wiser for worse.
Give
liz
    (take!
tommy)we
order a steak and they send us a pie(it's
try,
boys)
mine is yours

ask me the name of the moon in the man.
Up
sam
      (down!
alice)a
hole in the ocean will never be missed(it's
in,
girls)
yours is mine

either was deafer than neither was dumb.
Skip
fred
      (jump!
neddy)but
under the wonder is over the why(it's
now,
boys)
here we come

there are possibly 2½ or impossibly 3
individuals every several fat
thousand years. Expecting more would be
neither fantastic nor pathological but

dumb. The number of times a wheel turns
doesn't determine its roundness:if swallows tryst
in your barn be glad;nobody ever earns
anything,everything little looks big in a mist

and if(by Him Whose blood was for us spilled)
than all mankind something more small occurs
or something more distorting than socalled
civilization i'll kiss a stalinist arse

in hitler's window on wednesday next at 1
E.S.T. bring the kiddies let's all have fun

anyone lived in a pretty how town
(with up so floating many bells down)
spring summer autumn winter
he sang his didn't he danced his did.

Women and men(both little and small)
cared ror anyone not at all
they sowed their isn't they reaped their same
sun moon stars rain

children guessed(but only a few
and down they forgot as up they grew
autumn winter spring summer)
that noone loved him more by more

when by now and tree by leaf
she laughed his joy she cried his grief
bird by snow and stir by still
anyone's any was all to her

someones married their everyones
laughed their cryings and did their dance
(sleep wake hope and then)they
said their nevers they slept their dream

stars rain sun moon
(and only the snow can begin to explain
how children are apt to forget to remember
with up so floating many bells down)

one day anyone died i guess
(and noone stooped to kiss his face)
busy folk buried them side by side
little by little and was by was

all by all and deep by deep
and more by more they dream their sleep
noone and anyone earth by april
wish by spirit and if by yes.

Women and men(both dong and ding)
summer autumn winter spring
reaped their sowing and went their came
sun moon stars rain

the silently little blue elephant shyly(he was terri
bly
warped by his voyage from every to no)who
still stands still as found some lost thing(like a
curtain on which tiny the was painted in round
blue but quite now it's swirly and foldish so only through)the
little blue elephant at the zoo(jumbled
to queer this what that a here and
there a peers at you)has(elephant the blue)put some just
a now and now little the(on his quiet
head his magical shoulders him doll
self)hay completely thus or that wispily
is to say according to his perfect
satisfaction vanishing from a this world into bigger
much some out of(not visible to us)whom only his dream
ing own soul looks
and
the is all floatful and remembering

not time's how(anchored in what mountaining roots
of mere eternity)stupendous if
discoverably disappearing floats
at trillionworlded the ecstatic ease

with which vast my complexly wisdoming friend's
—a fingery treesoul onlying from serene
whom queries not suspected selves of space—
life stands gradually upon four minds

(out of some undering joy and overing grief
nothing arrives a so prodigious am
a so immediate is escorts us home
through never's always until absolute un

gulps the first knowledge of death's wandering guess)
while children climb their eyes to touch his dream

newlys of silence
(both an only

moon the with star

one moving are twilight
they beyond near)

girlest she slender

is cradling in joy her
flower than now

(softlying wisdoms

enter guess)
childmoon smile to

your breathing doll

33

one slipslouch twi
tterstamp
coon wid a plon
kykerplung
guit
ar
  (pleez make me glad)dis

dumdam slamslum slopp
idy wurl
sho am
wick
id id
ar
  (now heer we kum dearie)bud

hooz
gwine ter
hate
dad hurt
fool wurl no gal no
boy
   (day simbully loves id)fer

ids dare
pain dares un
no
budy elses un ids
dare dare
joy
  (eye kinely thank yoo)

my father moved through dooms of love
through sames of am through haves of give,
singing each morning out of each night
my father moved through depths of height

this motionless forgetful where
turned at his glance to shining here;
that if(so timid air is firm)
under his eyes would stir and squirm

newly as from unburied which
floats the first who,his april touch
drove sleeping selves to swarm their fates
woke dreamers to their ghostly roots

and should some why completely weep
my father's fingers brought her sleep:
vainly no smallest voice might cry
for he could feel the mountains grow.

Lifting the valleys of the sea
my father moved through griefs of joy;
praising a forehead called the moon
singing desire into begin

joy was his song and joy so pure
a heart of star by him could steer
and pure so now and now so yes
the wrists of twilight would rejoice

keen as midsummer's keen beyond
conceiving mind of sun will stand,
so strictly(over utmost him
so hugely)stood my father's dream

his flesh was flesh his blood was blood:
no hungry man but wished him food;
no cripple wouldn't creep one mile
uphill to only see him smile.

Scorning the pomp of must and shall
my father moved through dooms of feel;

his anger was as right as rain
his pity was as green as grain

septembering arms of year extend
less humbly wealth to foe and friend
than he to foolish and to wise
offered immeasurable is

proudly and(by octobering flame
beckoned)as earth will downward climb,
so naked for immortal work
his shoulders marched against the dark

his sorrow was as true as bread:
no liar looked him in the head;
if every friend became his foe
he'd laugh and build a world with snow.

My father moved through theys of we,
singing each new leaf out of each tree
(and every child was sure that spring
danced when she heard my father sing)

then let men kill which cannot share,
let blood and flesh be mud and mire,
scheming imagine,passion willed,
freedom a drug that's bought and sold

giving to steal and cruel kind,
a heart to fear,to doubt a mind,
to differ a disease of same,
conform the pinnacle of am

though dull were all we taste as bright,
bitter all utterly things sweet,
maggoty minus and dumb death
all we inherit,all bequeath

and nothing quite so least as truth
—i say though hate were why men breathe—
because my father lived his soul
love is the whole and more than all

you which could grin three smiles into a dead
house clutch between eyes emptiness toss one

at nobody shoulder and thick stickingly un

stride after glide massacre monday did
more)ask a lifelump buried by the star
nicked ends next among broken odds of yes
terday's tomorrow(than today can guess

or fears to dare whatever dares to fear)

i very humbly thank you which could grin
may stern particular Love surround your trite
how terrible selfhood with its hands and feet

(lift and may pitying Who from sharp soft worms

of spiralling why and out of black because
your absolute courage with its legs and arms

i say no world

can hold a you
shall see the not
because
and why but
(who
stood within his steam beginning and
began to sing all
here is hands machine no

good too quick i know this
suit you pay
a store too
much yes what
too much o much cheap
me i work i know i say i nave
not any
never
no vacation here

is hands is work since i am
born is good
but there this cheap this suit too
quick no suit there every
-thing
nothing i
say the
world not fit
you)he is

not(i say the world
yes any world is much
too not quite big enough to
hold one tiny this with
time's
more than
most how
immeasurable
anguish

pregnant one fearless
one good yes
completely kind
mindheart one true one generous child-
man
-god one eager
souldoll one
unsellable not buyable alive
one i say human being)one

goldberger

these children singing in stone a
silence of stone these
little children wound with stone
flowers opening for

ever these silently lit
tle children are petals
their song is a flower of
always their flowers

of stone are
silently singing
a song more silent
than silence these always

children forever
singing wreathed with singing
blossoms children of
stone with blossoming

eyes
know if a
lit tle
tree listens

forever to always children singing forever
a song made
of silent as stone silence of
song

love is the every only god

who spoke this earth so glad and big
even a thing all small and sad
man,may his mighty briefness dig

for love beginning means return
seas who could sing so deep and strong

one queerying wave will whitely yearn
from each last shore and home come young

so truly perfectly the skies
by merciful love whispered were,
completes its brightness with your eyes

any illimitable star

denied night's face
have shadowless they?
i bring you peace
the moon of day

predicted end
who never began
of god and fiend?
i give you man

extracted hate
from whispering grass?
joy in time shut
and starved on space?

love's murdered eye
dissected to mere
because and why?
take this whole tear.

By handless hints
do conjurers rule?
do mannikins
forbid the soul?

is death a whore
with life's disease
which quacks will cure
when pimps may please?

must through unstrange
synthetic now
true histories plunge?
rains a grey snow

of mothery same
rotting keen dream?
i rise which am
the sun of whom

a peopleshaped toomany-ness far too

and will it tell us who we are and will
it tell us why we dream and will it tell
us how we drink crawl eat walk die fly do?

a notalive undead too-nearishness

and shall we cry and shall we laugh and shall
entirely our doom steer his great small
wish into upward deepness of less fear
much than more climbing hope meets most despair?

all knowing's having and have is(you guess)
perhaps the very unkindest way to kill
each of those creatures called one's self so we'll

not have(but i imagine that yes is
the only living thing)and we'll make yes

up into the silence the green
silence with a white earth in it

you will(kiss me)go

out into the morning the young
morning with a warm world in it

(kiss me)you will go

on into the sunlight the fine
sunlight with a firm day in it

you will go(kiss me

down into your memory and
a memory and memory

i)kiss me(will go)

air,

be
comes
or

(a)

new
(live)
now

;&

th
(is no littler
th

an a:

fear no bigger
th
an a

hope)is

st
anding
st

a.r

enters give
whose lost is his found
leading love
whose heart is her mind)

supremely whole
uplifting the,
of each where all
was is to be

welcomes welcomes
her dreams his face
(her face his dreams
rejoice rejoice)

—opens the sun:
who music wear
burst icy known
swim ignorant fire

(adventuring
and time's dead which;
falling falling
both locked in each

down a thief by
a whore dragged goes
to meet her why
she his because

6

grEEn's d

an
cing on hollow was

young Up
floatingly clothes tumbledish
olD(with

sprouts o
ver and)a-
live
wanders remembe

r
ing per
F
ectl
y

crumb
ling eye
-holes oUt of whe
reful whom(leas

tly)
smiles the
infinite nothing

of
M

an

(sitting in a tree-)
o small you
sitting in a tree-

sitting in a treetop

riding on a greenest

riding on a greener
(o little i)
riding on a leaf

o least who
sing small thing
dance little joy

(shine most prayer)

mortals)

climbi
          ng i
          nto eachness begi
          n
dizzily
          swingthings
of speeds of
trapeze gush somersaults
open ing
             hes shes
&meet&
          swoop
                    fully is are ex
                                        quisite theys of re
turn
      a
      n
      d
fall which now drop who all dreamlike

(im

i am so glad and very
merely my fourth will cure
the laziest self of weary
the hugest sea of shore

so far your nearness reaches
a lucky fifth of you
turns people into eachs
and cowards into grow

our can'ts were born to happen
our mosts have died in more
our twentieth will open
wide a wide open door

we are so both and oneful
night cannot be so sky
sky cannot be so sunful
i am through you so i

what freedom's not some under's mere above
but breathing yes which fear will never no?
measureless our pure living complete love
whose doom is beauty and its fate to grow

shall hate confound the wise?doubt blind the brave?
does mask wear face?have singings gone to say?
here youngest selves yet younger selves conceive
here's music's music and the day of day

are worlds collapsing?any was a glove
but i'm and you are actual either hand
is when for sale?forever is to give
and on forever's very now we stand

nor a first rose explodes but shall increase
whole truthful infinite immediate us

A SELECTED LIST OF TITLES IN THE
Universal Library

LITERATURE, CRITICISM, DRAMA, AND POETRY

PSYCHOLOGY

OTHER TITLES OF INTEREST

THE TASTEMAKERS

By

RUSSELL LYNES

"TASTE," *says the author of this book, "is our personal pleasure, our private dilemma and our public facade."* THE TASTEMAKERS *is the lively story of the people and pressures that have shaped American taste for the last dozen decades.*

In a serious but witty and perceptive account, Mr. Lynes gives the battles of the tastemakers the dignity or humor they deserve — battles that are sometimes solemn and full of conviction, sometimes pompous, sometimes gay and frivolous. He reanimates — with all their original intensity and excitement — the battles of taste that account for our likes and dislikes today.

"*It is a highly original job, very sound in scholarship, very sagacious, and constantly amusing. ...The way he lightly transforms himself into an encyclopedia of American culture is delightful and a little breathtaking.*" BERNARD DEVOTO

"*It reads like the liveliest conversation of a wise friend—the sort of conversation one always wishes would find its way into a book.*" HERBERT AGAL

UL-54

WITH NAPOLEON IN RUSSIA

By

ARMAND DE CAULAINCOURT

IN AUGUST, 1933, an architect looking among the ruins of General Armand de Caulain-court's old chateau in Picardy, noticed a bat-tered iron chest in a pile of debris. On opening the chest he discovered the long-lost original manuscript of General de Caulaincourt's fabu-lous memoirs. Upon study, these memoirs turned out to be the most important discovery of Napoleonic materials in our time, for in them was a complete eye-witness account of how the Emperor planned and fought his greatest and most disastrous war—his invasion of Russia.

No book on Napoleon has more bearing on the events of today than this astounding chronicle of the struggle between the Emperor and the Czar. Here is revealed not only the thoughts and actions of the great Emperor as recorded by his most distinguished aide and confidant, but also startling insights into the enigmatic character and ways of the Russians, whom Caulaincourt knew well since he had been Ambassador to the court of St. Petersburg.

Scholars and students will find fascinating parallels in the events of then and now. They will also find within these pages the most vivid closeup of Napoleon that we possess, the pic-ture of a man considered a deity by many, possessed of the most remarkable qualities of leadership, yet prisoner of irrational obsessions that led him to defeat. UL-55

MADAME BOVARY

By

GUSTAVE FLAUBERT

MADAME BOVARY *has been called the first modern novel. Its influence on subsequent writers has been profound enough to warrant that description. Flaubert's magnificent achievement was to present a perfect perception of his characters with perfect objectivity. The result in* MADAME BOVARY *was a new kind of realism that shocked its first readers to the core. It remains for readers today just as impressive an experience. The tragedy of Emma Bovary is inexorable and belongs to the grand tradition of tragedy, but it is peculiarly modern, too. There is no appeal to the gods or to fate, no suggestion of a deus ex machina, however disguised. Step by step, with every action and motivation almost frighteningly real, Emma makes her own tragedy—and every other character is equally fully conceived. It is as if Flaubert had created whole people rather than characters of fiction and had then abandoned them to work out their own lives. But a closer examination reveals that this impression is achieved only through the most exquisitely painstaking craft.*

UL-57

NINE PLAYS OF CHEKOV

THE *delicate capture of a passing mood, the keen sympathy with the Hamlet in all human beings, the poignant probing of an overwhelming frustration—these are the elements which make up Chekov's dramatic vision of life. These plays of the twilight make Chekov, to the Russia of today, perhaps more alien than any other writer of the first rank, though he has been a major influence upon dramatists of the West.*

Perhaps Chekov's basic contribution to the stage can be summed up in the statement that he de-theatricalized the theatre. His plays end, as T. S. Eliot might say, not with a bang but a whimper. He demonstrates that tragedy can be as real in the slow wasting away of lives as in the great dramas of fore-destined catastrophe. He deals with human fate in a minor key.

That Chekov's dramas are of enduring appeal is proven by repeated revivals of his works. This volume, containing four of his major plays and five one-act masterpieces, also provides a valuable chronological table of the playwright's life and works. UL-59

THE ART OF LOVE

AND OTHER LOVE BOOKS OF

Ovid

Ovid's ART OF LOVE *has been called, in the words of the* Encyclopaedia Britannica, *"perhaps the most immoral book ever written by a man of genius." Its erotic brilliance appealed to the prevailing taste of the fashionable world of Ovid's day, an era of gross moral laxity, and has continued to fascinate readers for nearly 2000 years.*

Written in the elegant and graceful language of sophisticated Augustan Rome, the first two books of the ART OF LOVE *contain advice for the predatory male. The third book is devoted to aiding the female in her pursuit of the male. All three books are cast in the conventional form of the erotic Alexandrian elegy, but are graced with Ovid's unique wit.*

This volume also contains Ovid's other love books: THE LOVES, *in which he wrote about his mistress Corinna;* LOVE'S CURE, *a prescription for falling out of love; and* THE ART OF BEAUTY, *some further advice to the fair sex.*

It is interesting to note that of all the ancient poets, it was Ovid who made the most powerful impression on such writers as Marlowe, Spenser, Shakespeare, Milton and Dryden.

UL-61

CRIME AND PUNISHMENT

By

FYODOR DOSTOEVSKY

IT WOULD *probably be appalling to count the number of intelligent readers who have been put off from reading* Crime and Punishment *by its curious reputation as a classic of gloom — both classic and gloominess somehow suggest dullness. Nothing could be farther from Dostoevsky's masterpiece than the suggestion of dullness — disturbing, yes, even terrifying, but* Crime and Punishment *is more thrilling than any novel ever written to provide thrills.*

As Dorothy Brewster says in the introduction to this edition: "The plot, simple enough in outline, is full of breathless suspense and hair-raising episodes. It may be taken quite naively as one of the most thrilling of detective stories. Or just as naively — but more solemnly — as a Christian drama of sin and retribution...or into it may be read psychological, philosophical, and even metaphysical significance, to the limit of one's capacity for such speculation. On whatever levels of response it touches the reader's imagination, it is certain to be a disturbing experience." UL-63